This Book Belongs To

....

Date ...,...,.....

Made in the USA
Las Vegas, NV
22 September 2023

77967525R00069